FOR SINGERS WITH PIANO ACCOMPANIMENT

2	BICYCLE RACE
10	BOHEMIAN RHAPSODY
23	CRAZY LITTLE THING CALLED LOVE
32	DON'T STOP ME NOW
50	FAT BOTTOMED GIRLS
41	GOOD OLD-FASHIONED LOVER BOY
58	KILLER QUEEN
69	NOW I'M HERE
80	PLAY THE GAME
88	SAVE ME
94	SOMEBODY TO LOVE
114	WE ARE THE CHAMPIONS
107	YOU'RE MY BEST FRIEND

Photo: Ian Dickson/Contributor/Getty Images

ISBN 978-1-4950-8937-4

For all works contained herein:
Unauthorized copying, arranging, adapting, recording, Internet posting, public performance,
or other distribution of the music in this publication is an infringement of copyright.
Infringers are liable under the law.

Visit Hal Leonard Online at
www.halleonard.com

Contact Us:
Hal Leonard
7777 West Bluemound Road
Milwaukee, WI 53213
Email: info@halleonard.com

In Europe contact:
Hal Leonard Europe Limited
Distribution Centre, Newmarket Road
Bury St Edmunds, Suffolk, IP33 3YB
Email: info@halleonardeurope.com

In Australia contact:
Hal Leonard Australia Pty. Ltd.
4 Lentara Court
Cheltenham, Victoria, 3192 Australia
Email: info@halleonard.com.au

BICYCLE RACE

Words and Music by
FREDDIE MERCURY

Fast Rock (Half-time feel)

Copyright © 1978 Queen Music Ltd.
All Rights Administered by Sony/ATV Music Publishing LLC, 424 Church Street, Suite 1200, Nashville, TN 37219
International Copyright Secured   All Rights Reserved

(You say coke,) I say caine. (You say John,) I say Wayne. (Hot dog!)

I say cool it, man, I don't wan - na be the Pres - i - dent of A -

BOHEMIAN RHAPSODY

Words and Music by
FREDDIE MERCURY

Slowly

(Is this the real life? Is this just fan-ta-sy? ___ Caught in a land-slide, no es-

With pedal

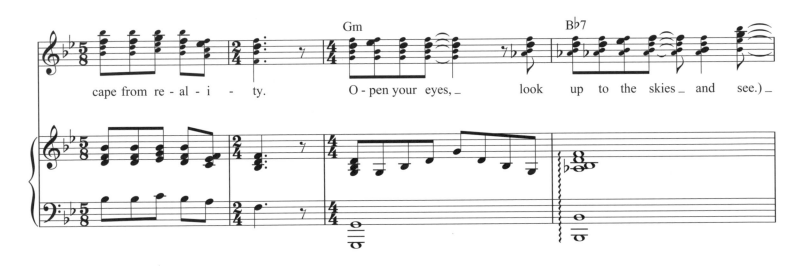

cape from re-al-i-ty. O-pen your eyes, ___ look up to the skies ___ and see.) ___

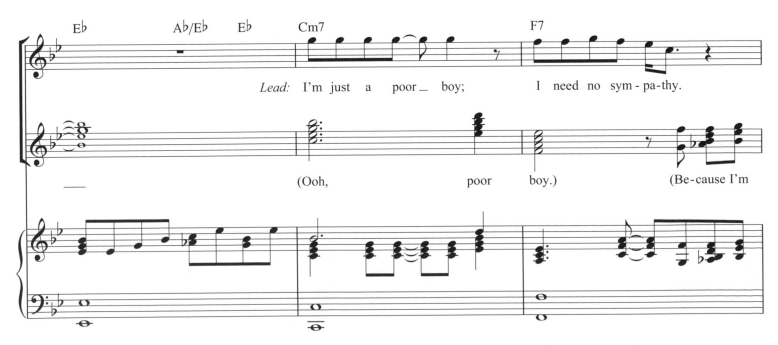

Lead: I'm just a poor ___ boy; I need no sym-pa-thy.

(Ooh, poor boy.) (Be-cause I'm

Copyright © 1975 Queen Music Ltd.
Copyright Renewed
All Rights Administered by Sony/ATV Music Publishing LLC, 424 Church Street, Suite 1200, Nashville, TN 37219
International Copyright Secured   All Rights Reserved

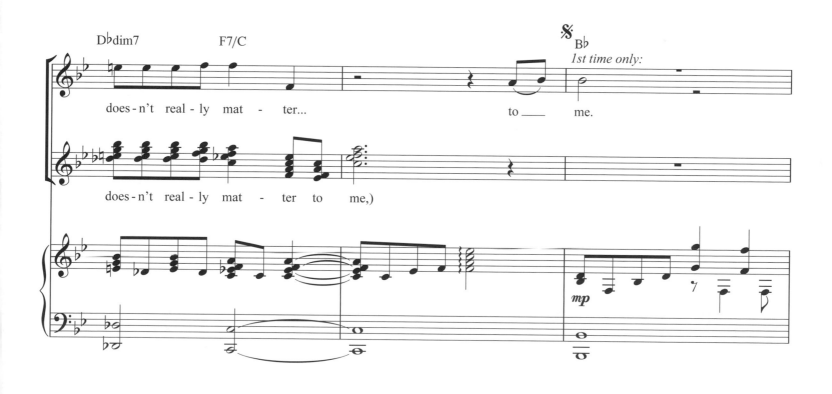

I'm not back a-gain___ this time to-mor - row, car-ry on, car-ry

D.S. al Coda

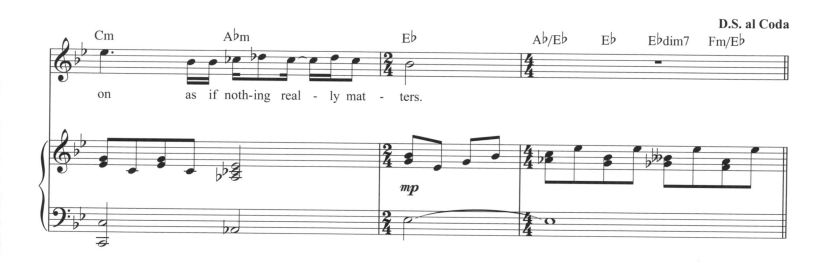

on as if noth-ing real - ly mat - ters.

CODA

Ma - ma, _____ ooh, _____ (An - y way the wind blows.)

(Ooh.) _____

I don't wan-na die. _ I some-times wish I'd nev-er been born at all. _

(Ooh, _____

ooh, _____

_ Guitar solo ad lib.

ooh.) _____

Twice as fast

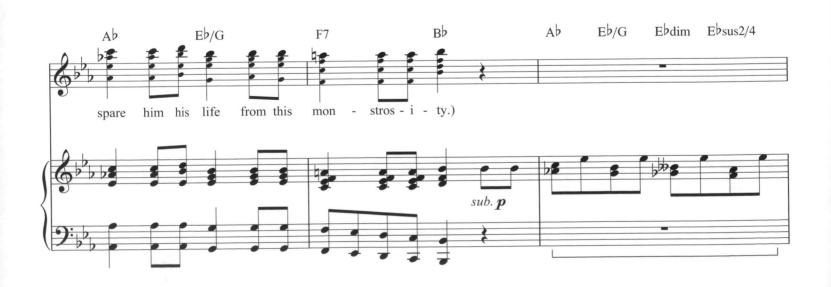

Heavy Shuffle

So you think you can

stone me and spit in my eye?

So ___ you think you ___ can love me ___ and leave me ___ to

die? _____ Oh, ba - by, _____

can't ___ do this to ___ me, ba - by. _____

Just got-ta get out, ___ just got-ta get right out ___ of here. _____

CRAZY LITTLE THING CALLED LOVE

Words and Music by
FREDDIE MERCURY

Copyright © 1979 Queen Music Ltd.
All Rights Administered by Sony/ATV Music Publishing LLC, 424 Church Street, Suite 1200, Nashville, TN 37219
International Copyright Secured   All Rights Reserved

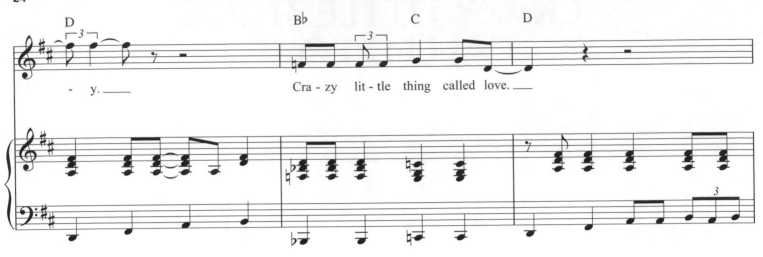

Cra - zy lit - tle thing called love.

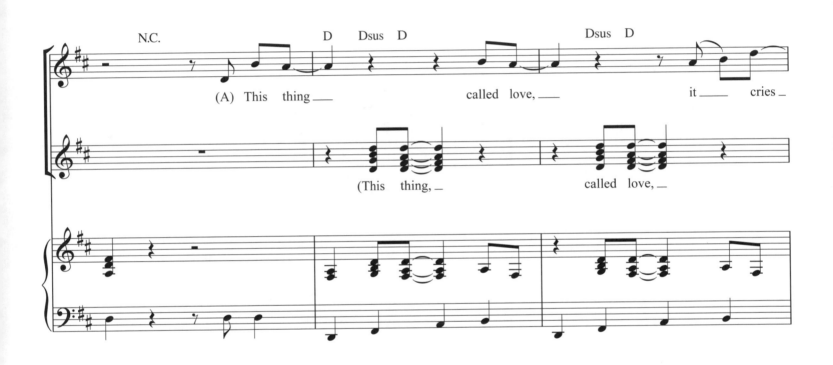

(A) This thing ___ called love, ___ it ___ cries ___

(This thing, ___ called love, ___

in a cra - dle all night. It swings, ___ it ___ jives, ___

like a ba - by.) (Oo, hoo. ___

shakes all ___ o - ver like a jel - ly - fish, ___ I kind - a

Oo, hoo.) ___   (Oo, ___ I kind - a

like it. ___   Cra - zy lit - tle thing called love. ___

like it.)

There goes my ba - by. ___   She

back - seat, hitch - hike, ___ and take a long ride on my

mot - or - bike ___ un - til I'm read - y. Cra - zy lit - tle thing called love. ___

Instrumental solo

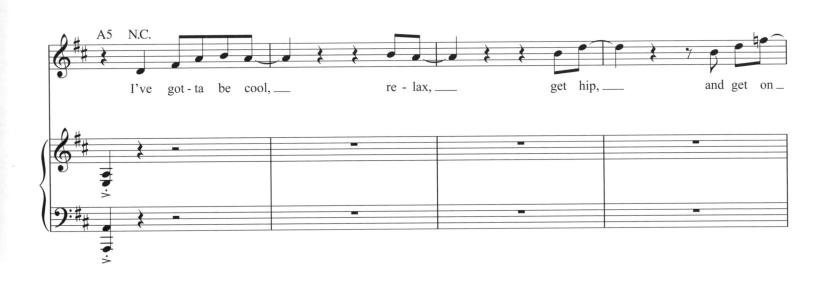

take a long ride on my mot-or-bike __ un-til I'm read-y.

Mm. ____

Read-y, Fred-die.)

Cra-zy lit-tle thing called love. __

This thing __

__ called love, ____ I ____ just ____ can't

han - dle it. ___ This thing ___ called love, ___ I ___ must ___ get

'round to it, ___ I ain't read - y. Cra - zy lit - tle thing called love. ___

(Ooh, _____ cra - zy lit - tle thing called love.) ___

Cra - zy lit - tle thing called love. ___

(Yeah, yeah.)

DON'T STOP ME NOW

Words and Music by
FREDDIE MERCURY

Copyright © 1978 Queen Music Ltd.
All Rights Administered by Sony/ATV Music Publishing LLC, 424 Church Street, Suite 1200, Nashville, TN 37219
International Copyright Secured   All Rights Reserved

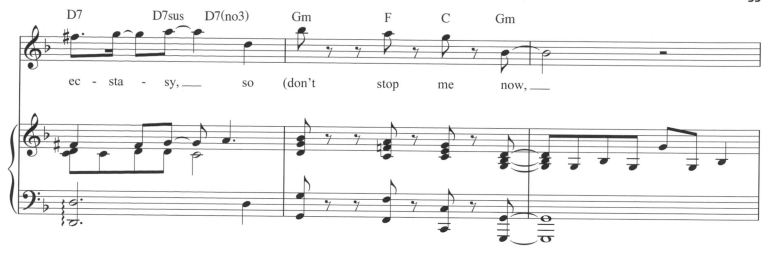

ec - sta - sy, ___ so (don't stop me now, ___

Moderately fast

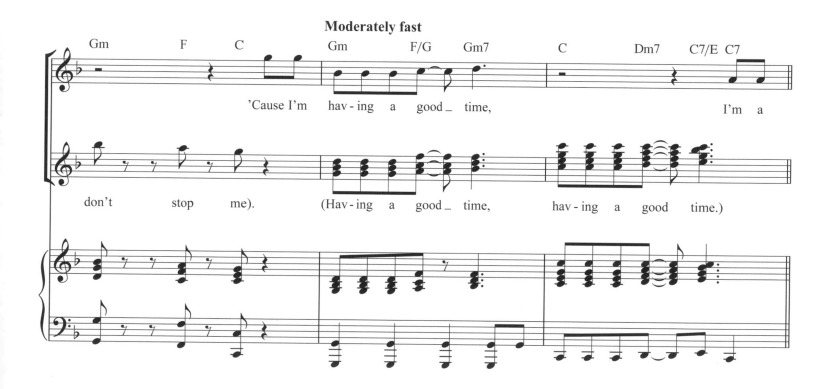

'Cause I'm hav - ing a good ___ time,   I'm a
don't   stop   me).   (Hav - ing a good ___ time,   hav - ing a good   time.)

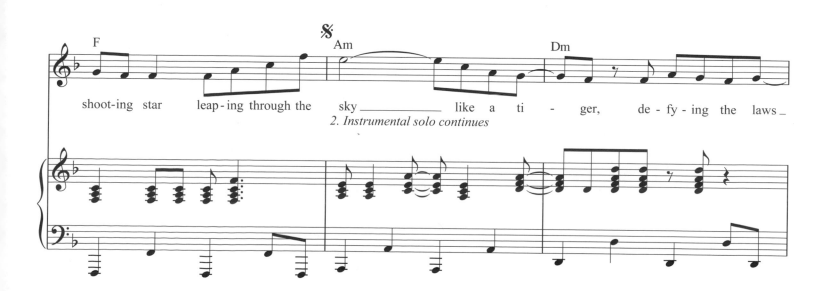

shoot - ing star   leap - ing through the   sky _____ like a ti - ger,   de - fy - ing the laws __
2. Instrumental solo continues

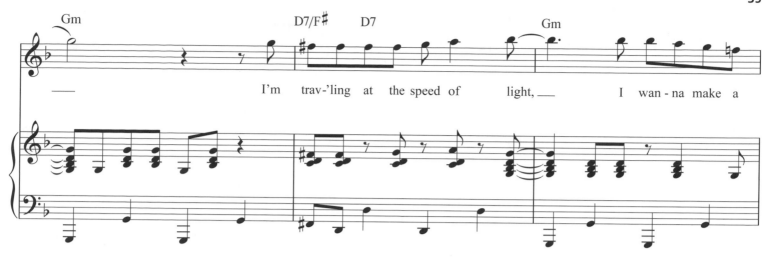

I'm trav-'ling at the speed of light, ___ I wan-na make a

su - per - son - ic man out of you. ___

(su - per - son - ic man out of you.) ___ (Don't stop me now.) _

I'm hav-ing such a good time, I'm hav-ing a ball. __

stop me, don't stop me, ooh, ooh, ooh.) *I like it!* Don't stop me, don't stop me.) Have a

8va F
div.
D.S. al Coda

good time, good time.
(Don't stop me, don't stop me. *Instrumental solo ad lib.* Oh!)

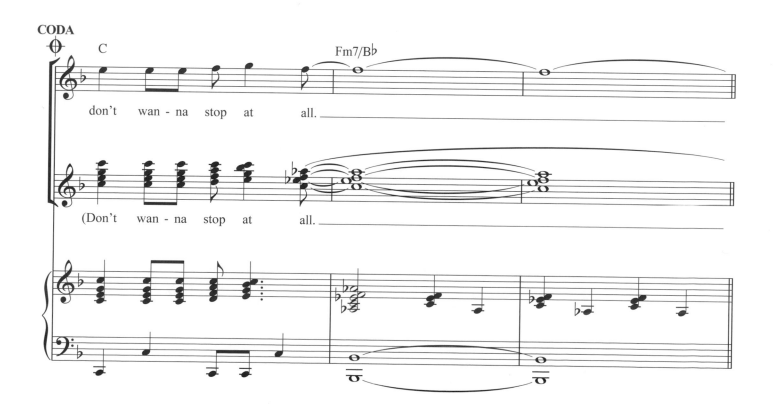

CODA
C Fm7/B♭

don't wan - na stop at all.

(Don't wan - na stop at all.

Moderately slow

La da da da da, _____ da da da ___ ha. _____ Ha _ da

da, _ ha _ ha ha. ____ Ha da da. ____ La da da. _____

Fadeout begins

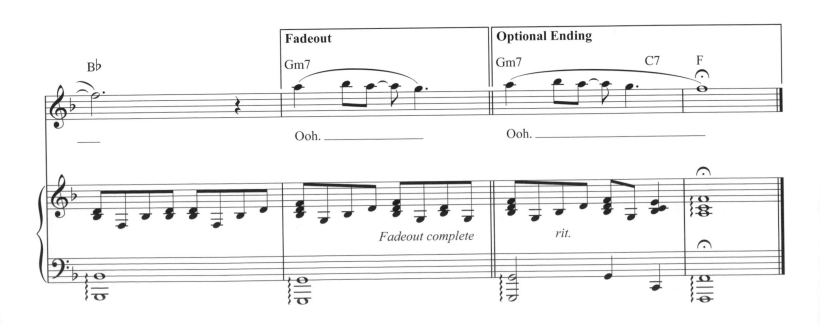

Fadeout

Optional Ending

___ Ooh. _____ Ooh. _____

Fadeout complete   *rit.*

GOOD OLD-FASHIONED LOVER BOY

Words and Music by
FREDDIE MERCURY

Moderately (16th-note Shuffle)

I can dim the lights _ and sing you songs _ full of sad _ things;

we can do the tan - go just for two; I can ser - e - nade _ and gent - ly

play on your heart _ strings, be your Val - en - ti - no, just for you. _

(Ooh.) _

Copyright © 1976, 1977 Queen Music Ltd.
Copyright Renewed
All Rights Administered by Sony/ATV Music Publishing LLC, 424 Church Street, Suite 1200, Nashville, TN 37219
International Copyright Secured   All Rights Reserved

Ooh, love, ooh, lov - er

(Ooh, love, ooh, lov - er

boy, what - cha do - ing to - night, ___ hey boy? ___ set

boy, _____ ooh, hey boy?) ___

my a - larm, ___ turn on ___ my charm; ___ that's be - cause I'm a good old - fash - ioned lov - er boy. ___

Solo ends

Din - ing at the Ritz, __ we'll meet at nine __

mp

__ pre - cise - ly. I will pay the bill, __ you taste the wine. __

(One, two, three, four, five, six, sev - en, eight, nine o'- clock.)

Driv - ing back in style in my sa - loon, _

_ do quite nice - ly; _ just take me back to yours, _ that will be fine. _

Come on and get it. Ooh, love,
(Ooh, love,

(There he goes a - gain;

FAT BOTTOMED GIRLS

Words and Music by
BRIAN MAY

Moderately slow

Aw, you gon-na take me home to-night? Aw, down be-side

that red fire light? Aw, you gon-na

let it all hang out? Fat bot-tomed girls, you make the rock-in' world go

Copyright © 1978 Queen Music Ltd.
All Rights Administered by Sony/ATV Music Publishing LLC, 424 Church Street, Suite 1200, Nashville, TN 37219
International Copyright Secured   All Rights Reserved

KILLER QUEEN

Words and Music by
FREDDIE MERCURY

Copyright © 1974 Queen Music Ltd.
Copyright Renewed
All Rights Administered by Sony/ATV Music Publishing LLC, 424 Church Street, Suite 1200, Nashville, TN 37219
International Copyright Secured   All Rights Reserved

sa - tia - ble in ap - pe - tite. ___ Wan - na try? ___

(Wan - na try?) ___

To a - void com - pli - ca - tions, ___ she

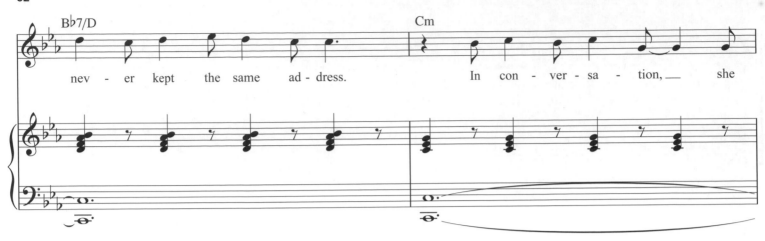

never kept the same address. In con-ver-sa-tion, she

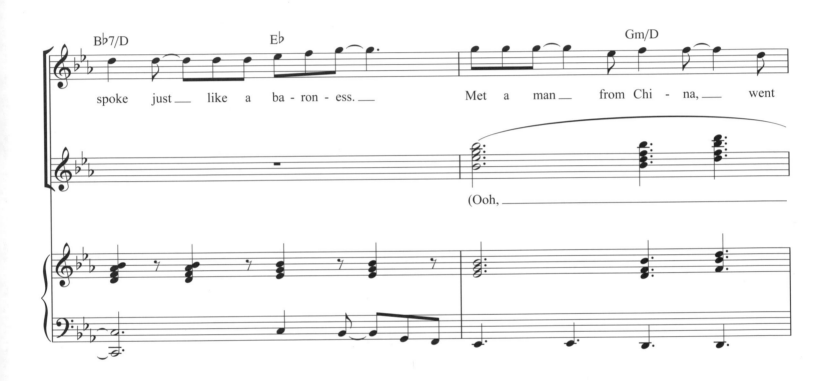

spoke just like a ba-ron-ess. Met a man from Chi-na, went

(Ooh,

down to Gei-sha Mi-nah, but then a-gain in-ci-den-t'ly if you're

A kill-er, a kill-er, she's a

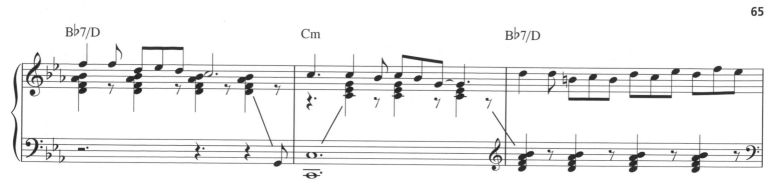

Solo ends Drop of a hat, she's as will-ing as, ___ play-ful as a pus-sy-cat; ___ then

(Ooh, ___

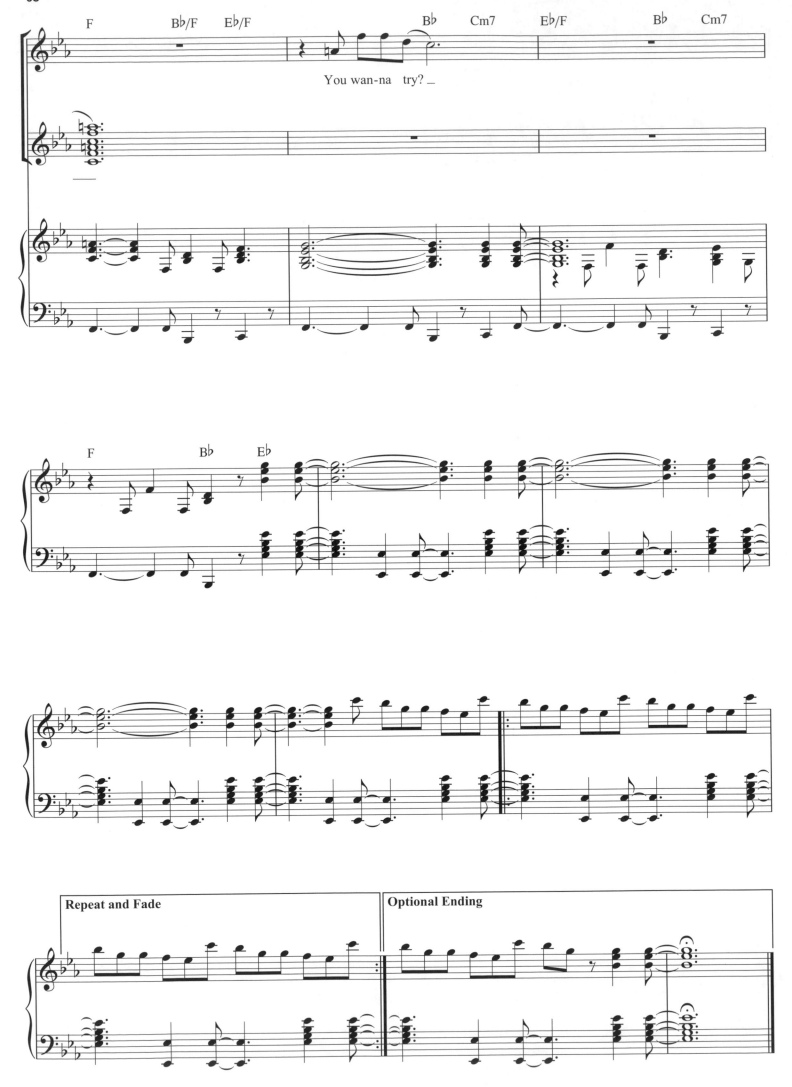

You wan-na try? _

Repeat and Fade

Optional Ending

NOW I'M HERE

Words and Music by
BRIAN MAY

Copyright © 1974 Queen Music Ltd.
Copyright Renewed
All Rights Administered by Sony/ATV Music Publishing LLC, 424 Church Street, Suite 1200, Nashville, TN 37219
International Copyright Secured   All Rights Reserved

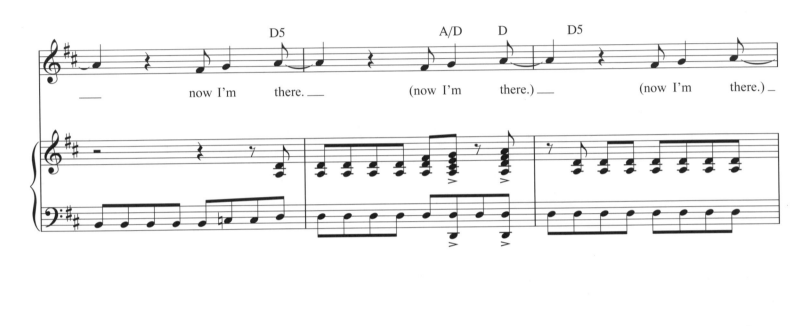

(Don't I love ___ you ___ so.)

Instrumental solo

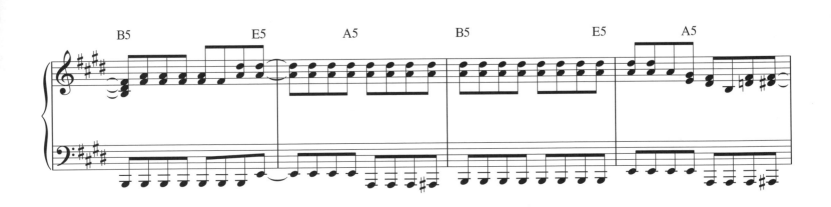

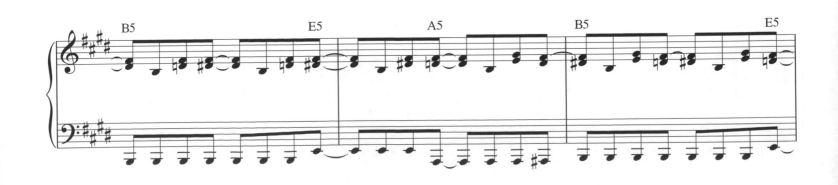

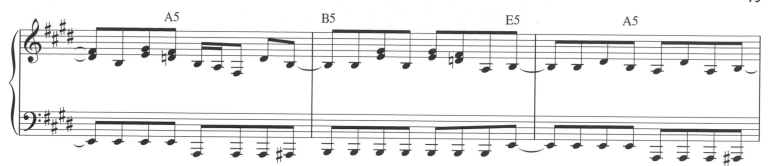

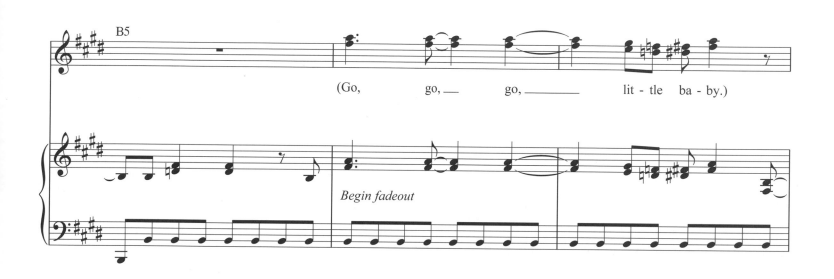

(Go, go, — go, ——— lit - tle ba - by.)

Begin fadeout

(Instrumental solo continues ad lib.)

Repeat and Fade   **Optional Ending**

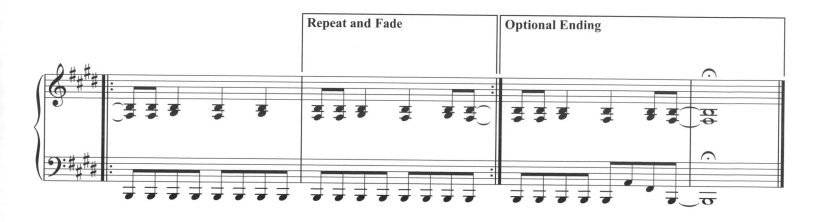

PLAY THE GAME

Words and Music by
FREDDIE MERCURY

O-pen up your mind and let me step in-side. ___

Rest your wea-ry head ___ and let your heart de-cide. ___ It's so eas - y
(eas - y)

when you know ___ the rules. ___ It's so eas - y;
(eas - y)

Copyright © 1980 Queen Music Ltd.
All Rights Administered by Sony/ATV Music Publishing LLC, 424 Church Street, Suite 1200, Nashville, TN 37219
International Copyright Secured   All Rights Reserved

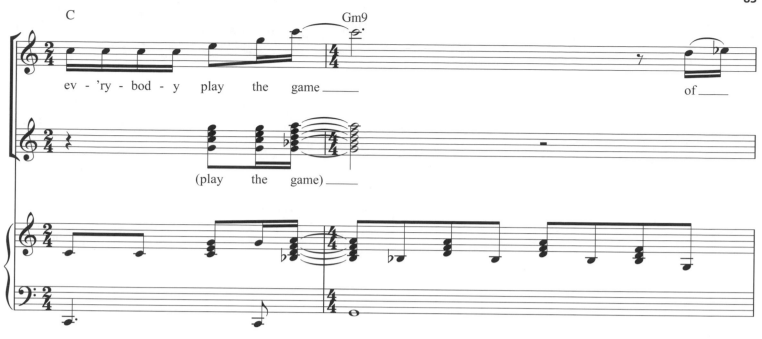

ev - 'ry - bod - y play the game _____ of _____

(play the game) _____

love. ___ Ooh, _____ ah. ___

My game of love has just be - gun. Love runs from my

(Love runs from my

SAVE ME

Words and Music by
BRIAN MAY

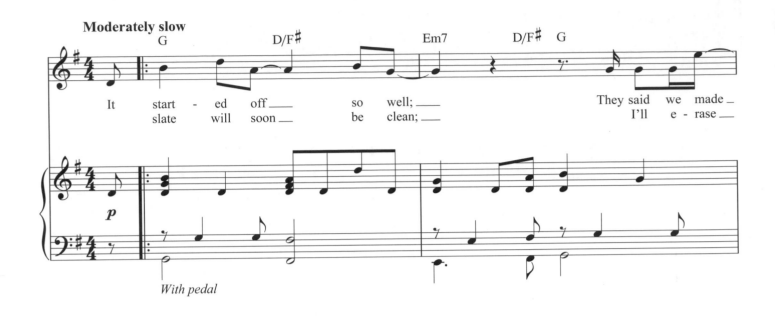

It start - ed off __ so well; __ They said we made __ I'll e - rase __

slate will soon __ be clean; __

__ a per - fect pair. __ I clothed my - self __ in your glo -

__ the mem - o - ries, __ to start a - gain __ with some -

ry and your love. How I loved __ you! How I cried! __ The

- bod - y new. Was it all wast - ed, all that love? __ I

Copyright © 1980 Queen Music Ltd.
All Rights Administered by Sony/ATV Music Publishing LLC, 424 Church Street, Suite 1200, Nashville, TN 37219
International Copyright Secured   All Rights Reserved

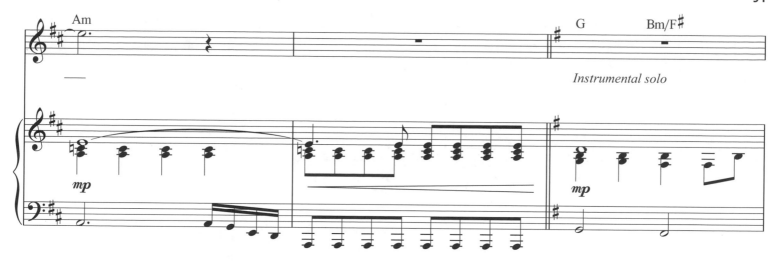

Instrumental solo

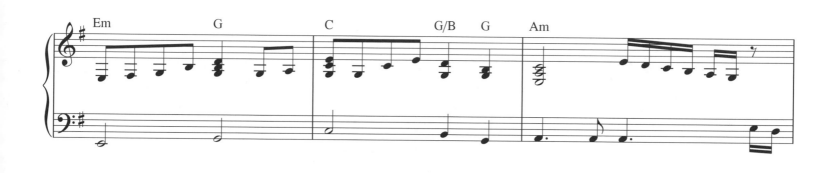

Each night I cry; — I still be - lieve the lie. — I'll love —

you __ un - til I die. __ (Save me, save me,
Instrumental solo

save me.) __ (Yeah,
Solo ends

Yeah, __ oh __ save __ me. Don't let me face my life __ a -

save me, save me, ooh.) __

SOMEBODY TO LOVE

Words and Music by
FREDDIE MERCURY

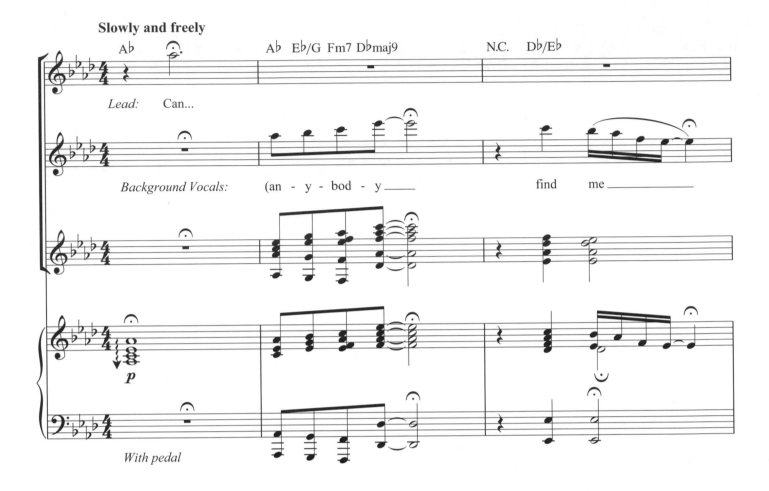

Copyright © 1976 Queen Music Ltd.
Copyright Renewed
All Rights Administered by Sony/ATV Music Publishing LLC, 424 Church Street, Suite 1200, Nashville, TN 37219
International Copyright Secured   All Rights Reserved

Each morn ing I get up, I die a lit-tle; can't

bare - ly stand __ on my feet; ___ take a look _____ in the mir-ror and cry, ___

(Take a look at your - self in ____ the mir - ror and

"Lord, what-cha do-in' to me?" _ I have spent all my years in be-liev - in' You, but I

cry, ____ yeah, ___ yeah. Ooh, _____ be-liev - in' You, I

YOU'RE MY BEST FRIEND

Words and Music by
JOHN DEACON

Copyright © 1975 Queen Music Ltd.
Copyright Renewed
All Rights Administered by Sony/ATV Music Publishing LLC, 424 Church Street, Suite 1200, Nashville, TN 37219
International Copyright Secured   All Rights Reserved

WE ARE THE CHAMPIONS

Words and Music by
FREDDIE MERCURY

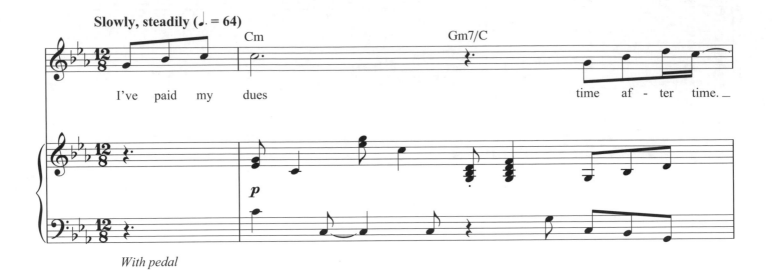

Copyright © 1977 Queen Music Ltd.
Copyright Renewed
All Rights Administered by Sony/ATV Music Publishing LLC, 424 Church Street, Suite 1200, Nashville, TN 37219
International Copyright Secured   All Rights Reserved

fame and for - tune and ev -'ry - thing that goes with it; I thank you

all. But it's been __ no bed of ros - es, ___ no plea-sure

cruise. I con - sid - er it a

chal - lenge be - fore the whole hu - man race, and I nev - er lose! ___

(And I need just go

MORE GREAT VOCAL PUBLICATIONS FROM

Music Minus One

The Music Minus One recordings feature world-class musicians and orchestras from the United States, Vienna, Bulgaria, and elsewhere in Europe. The recordings allow the vocalist to listen to the full recording, and then pan the recording to remove the vocalist so they can step in and sing the lead.

THE BEATLES
SING 8 FAB FOUR HITS
00236167 Book/Online Audio $19.99

**BRAHMS SONGS –
VOCAL ACCOMPANIMENTS**
MUSIC MINUS ONE LOW VOICE
00400545 Book/Online Audio $14.99

**BRAHMS SONGS –
VOCAL ACCOMPANIMENTS**
MUSIC MINUS ONE HIGH VOICE
00400544 Book/Online Audio $14.99

CHILDREN'S SONGS SING-ALONGS
00152966 Book/2-CD Pack $14.99

CHRISTMAS MEMORIES
00400043 Book/CD Pack $14.99

**CHRISTMAS STANDARDS
FOR FEMALE SINGERS**
00242589 Book/Online Audio $16.99

DEAR EVAN HANSEN
by Benj Pasek and Justin Paul
00241594 Book/Online Audio $22.99

**DISNEY SONGS FOR
FEMALE SINGERS**
10 ALL-TIME FAVORITES WITH FULLY-
ORCHESTRATED BACKING TRACKS
00248822 Book/Online Audio $19.99

**DISNEY SONGS FOR
MALE SINGERS**
10 ALL-TIME FAVORITES WITH FULLY
ORCHESTRATED BACKING TRACKS
00248823 Book/Online Audio $19.99

THE GREATEST SHOWMAN
by Benj Pasek and Justin Paul
00269778 Book/Online Audio $24.99

HAMILTON
10 SELECTIONS FROM THE HIT MUSICAL
00190974 Book/Online Audio $16.99

LA LA LAND
6 SELECTIONS FROM THE HIT MOVIE
00222221 Book/Online Audio $22.99

**LUSH AND LOVELY STANDARDS
WITH ORCHESTRA**
SONGS IN THE STYLE OF BARBRA STREISAND
00147460 Book/CD Pack $14.99

**SING THE SONGS OF
JOHNNY MERCER, VOLUME 1
(FOR MALE VOCALISTS)**
SINGER'S CHOICE – PROFESSIONAL TRACKS
FOR SERIOUS SINGERS
00138902 Book/CD Pack $14.99

**SING THE SONGS OF
JOHNNY MERCER, VOLUME 2
(FOR FEMALE VOCALISTS)**
SINGER'S CHOICE – PROFESSIONAL TRACKS
FOR SERIOUS SINGERS
00142485 Book/CD Pack $14.99

ONE MOMENT IN TIME
00152963 Book/CD Pack $14.99

THE PHANTOM OF THE OPERA
by Andrew Lloyd Webber
00244102 Book/Online Audio $22.99

ELVIS PRESLEY
00279891 Book/Online Audio $19.99

ED SHEERAN
00275772 Book/Online Audio $19.99

TAYLOR SWIFT
SING 8 FAVORITES
00223015 Book/Online Audio $19.99

**TEN MORE CLASSIC VOCAL
STANDARDS**
00400601 Book/CD Pack $14.99

**TWELVE CLASSIC VOCAL
STANDARDS**
00400598 Book/CD Pack $14.99

**WEEKEND WARRIORS, SET LIST-
LADIES' NIGHT SINGER'S
SONGBOOK**
MUSIC MINUS ONE FEMALE VOCALIST
00121505 Book/CD Pack $14.99

Disney characters and artwork © Disney Enterprises, Inc.

HAL•LEONARD®
www.halleonard.com
Prices, contents, and availability subject to change without notice.

To see a full listing of
Music Minus One publications, visit
www.halleonard.com/MusicMinusOne

0718